CATCHING THE LIGHT

MARK ROPER

LAGAN PRESS
BELFAST
1996

Acknowledgements are due to the editors of the following,
in which some of these poems first appeared:
*Cyphers, Foolscap, Force 10, Fortnight, The Independent, North, Oxford Poetry,
Other Poetry, Poetry Ireland, Poetry Wales, Rialto, Riverine, Smith Knoll,
Waterford Review, Windows Selection.*

Published by
Lagan Press
PO Box 110 BT12 4AB, Belfast

The publishers wish to acknowledge the financial assistance
of the Arts Council of Northern Ireland in the production of this book.

A catalogue record of this book is available from the British Library.

ISBN: 1 873687 478
Author: Roper, Mark
Title: Catching the Light
Format: Paperback (138 mm x 210 mm)
1996

Cover Image: Three Windows for Anne Sexton (1973) by T.P. Flanagan
Design: December Publications
Set in Palatino
Printed by Noel Murphy Printing, Belfast

for Carmel, Catriona, Jean, Kerry and Pat
thanks to Barrie and Eilis for the Commodore

Contents

Angel 11

The Last Tiger in Piltown 13

Safe and Satisfactory 15

Suzy 16

Wood 18

North Coast 19

Edgeways 20

The Census 21

You 22

The Adventure Centre 24

The Cup of Tea 25

The Silence Cloth 26

To the Comma 28

Here 29

Breaking Ground 30

The Landmark 31

Dunmore Cave 32

Bawnreigh Slate Quarry 33

Clay Pipes 35

Main de Gloire 36

Palm 37

Red Handed 38

Herons 39

Halcyon 41

Svala! Svala! 42

Snipe 43

Consider the Lilies 45

November 46

Marsh Marigolds 47

Appetite 48

No Problem 49

The Masked Walkers 50

Port Sunlight 51

The New Light 52

Honey 53
The Takabuti Mummy 54
The Sun Room 56
Letter from Ladakh 57
Catching the Light 59
Unbecoming 60
Prayer 61
Instinct 62
Practice 63
What the Deer Said 65
To Silence 66
Scythe 67

ANGEL

An angel showed me its wing
in a field at the back of the house.
It was leathery inside, vein-knotted,
welted with stitchmarks and scars.
There were fleas in the feathers
which it made me catch and crush.
You could feel the shafts buried
deep in the skin, like great nails.

I smuggled food, ointment for the wings.
Perhaps my father wouldn't have minded;
it was too dangerous to ask. Everyone
said we'd be better off without them.
There was talk of showtrials, mass graves,
of the need to be rid of them forever.
Some had appeared on TV, denying
they could fly, confessing to sexual acts.

The angel said it had almost been caught.
'I sheltered in a church, but they refuse
to acknowledge us, they're striking us
from the record, saying we never existed.'
It stayed for a month, sleeping by day.
I got used to the silhouette,
like that of a giant owl or moth
beating through the woods at dusk.

At first I took the blame when things
began to disappear from the house.
When my father's watch went missing
he forced the truth out of me.

[11]

I remember ragged shadows on the ground,
reassuring hands on my shoulder, voices
telling me I'd done the right thing,
quiet orders given to the dogs;

how the angel stood there in the lights
and just before all hell broke loose
how it opened its mouth and sang,
small tongue oddly neat and clean.
And the awful beauty of that song,
how it seemed to have nothing
to do with anything, seemed even then
to have forgotten where it came from.

THE LAST TIGER IN PILTOWN

Though he's lent his name to
a wide range of jungle products,
he hasn't had to hunt in years.
He's sticking to the road now,
walking to numb a cramp,
stopping for a paper at Anthony's
or a pint of milk at O'Keeffe's.

When they needed to claim
he was making a comeback
they'd film him on the prowl,
let him stalk and savage
what seemed to be a goat.
He became too easily recognised,
advertising slipped into
the skin-pattern, the undergrowth.

Worst thing was the breeding.
In the absence of a female
they tried all kinds of substitute.
Most burst when he got excited.
These days he's just not up
to it, has frequent headaches.

But every inch is photographed,
genetic coding's nearly cracked,
a decent imitation should be
widely available soon.

He can't remember himself
which bits are meant to be real.
This afternoon negotiations
over the new winter skin.

Tomorrow a French TV crew,
another offer to found a religion,
the old attempt to finish his memoirs.

Often he's not there at all.
Just the door open, radio on,
vibration of stripes in a chair.
That fuel-shock, shimmer of air
above slightly parting grass.

SAFE AND SATISFACTORY

After the ceremony Pilate thanked the sponsors,
Thorncraft, Golgotha Joinery, Vinegar Joe's.
He went on to affirm the safety of the conviction,
stressing the appalling vista of a Pharisee lie,
but at his club that night he confided to a crony:
'It was the vintners, you understand, that trick
with the water. Threat to their livelihood.
Couldn't have that. Now if he'd turned wine into water!
All do that, eh! Do it meself in a minute. Fancy another?'

He ordered dinner and made a few notes on his napkin.
'Personal appearance, quick, for him. Him.
Then South America. Hold back Cross, let demand
build—market as individual splinters! Signed?
Maybe not. Promote disciples; different haircuts,
bit of conflict. Get some pictures done. Fax contract
to Tarsus.' He ordered a taxi, smiling as the driver
commented on the silence, on the weird sunset.

SUZY

This is your face.
On the window glass,
look, your face.
It's you, believe me.

That's a tree,
that's a car and
here comes mother,
piled with presents
you can't use.

Father? Drunk down
at the rugby club, boasting
how much he loves you?

You were an oracle.
They took each spasm
for a smile,
each grunt for speech.
They're wiser now,
foundered on the rock
of your silence.

Save them. Now's the time.
See it's alright
when you're a child.
Grown-ups are harder.
Grown-up piss and shit
is not so easy to love.
And then there's your sex.

Please respond.
Sit up on my shoulders.
Grip the ceiling bar tight.

Be a monkey, be a bird.
Let your fingers
trigger your tongue.

When the team of four comes
to pattern your limbs,
get up and walk away.
Turn on the telly.
Demand more jam.

Though the team of four is
hard to raise these days.

Lie down on the waterbed.
Be a fish in a warm sea.
Rise
to the occasion.

Don't just sit there.

WOOD

The nice man who asked me to help him find golf balls
nursed a purple driver under his mac. By day
Teds oiled their quiffs and cycle chains; at night
they set fire to the rowing boats. The lake was lined
with broken glass. I cut my foot down to the bone,
watched a toad swallow the bleb of flesh. It wasn't
very good in the dark dark wood, just like Noddy said.

My mother warned I'd get an accent, promised me a tin foot
if I ever went again. Too late. I was in, I had mates.
They mocked my muscles, smaller than sparrows' kneecaps,
but I was alright. My sister warned me Dogger's mother
had had five children since his dad went to jail.
That didn't seem to matter. Until I told Dogger.
Though he chased me all the way I just made it home,
slamming the front door on him, thanking my lucky stars
until the letterbox began to belch dogshit and sticks.

I shouted for my father, left him to sort it out,
stumped off down the hall to my own tinny applause.

NORTH COAST

You'd no time for Amble harbour's broken silvers,
that nitid jigsaw simmering beyond the houses,
rickety piers crosshatching the collapse and curl.

You'd eyes only for sea coal, the smooth tablets
among the stones. Their salty flare. Free fuel.
You were head down on a fifties winter day

hunting those nuggets, hoping no one was watching,
hating the ocean's cold charity, your own need.
As for the dolphin out in the bay, we could keep it,

and its promise of unconditional love, and the sign
advising just how not to love it back. You'd started
on the unemployed geordies, how they were stripping

the suburbs of videos to fund their Spanish holidays,
how their mining ancestors beat up yours, farmworkers
who dared to break their strike. No surprise then

at Newton your blindness to the wind-shaved waves,
the castle's moth-eaten silhouette, the auguries
of knot and dunlin. You, you'd homed in again,

on the square of fishing cottages; bijou lovenests
now but once you insisted so far from anywhere
women must have stood at their windows in tears,

facing into a day of washing, children and no company
and bound to endure such isolation forever.

EDGEWAYS

Lift up the town you'd find him
hanging on, part of the archive,
an anchored afterthought.

Where most leave, on the quay,
shoes or bag to mark that point
of departure, he fastened

a rope, one end to an ankle,
the other to a bollard
before taking the plunge.

Whether he intended to save
his family the torment
of long searching for his body,

whether he just wanted
for the first and last time
to draw attention to himself

is not known. Whatever,
he made no mistake, so lost
in his own life there seemed

no way back, no breadcrumb trail,
no samaritan line. He's still there,
under the town in parenthesis:

who took politeness
to an extreme or who finally
got a word in edgeways.

THE CENSUS

'I don't care what you find,'
said the sergeant, handing
us the forms. 'Just don't
find me any more land.'

The level-crossing gate
hadn't opened in years.
Bolts had rusted solid.
One might wait forever.

Last night you dreamt about
the room again, the room
inside the room. 'Perhaps,'
you said, 'It dreamt about me.'

We found the train in a field.
Our great eyes filled up
the windows as we stared in
on the tiny frozen passengers.

YOU

We weren't sympathetic, were we?
Our lines were always engaged.
We don't hear much from you lately—
are you losing hope now we've aged?

You can still make your absence felt—
at the meal-table, too long a pause.
Pampered cats. Too neat a garden.
In such ways you plead your cause.

One time at least you got close—
by mistake, as they say it should be.
You must have thought this was it,
at last the passage was free.

You'd begun to head towards land,
we stood by prepared to receive.
In the end it was all a mix-up
and face it, we were relieved.

We're not half the people we should be.
Too lightly we walk on this earth.
Cowards, selfish, your voice whispers.
Be devils. Be parents. Give birth.

I'll stop your world from shrinking.
I'll save you from dying out.
I'll console the surviving partner—
it's got to be worth trying out.

No decision is final of course,
believe me your hearing's been fair
but it looks as if this is the verdict:
might have been but never were.

[22]

Don't hold your absence against us,
you have your place in the parade,
you'll be there forever between us,
a difference we never made.

THE ADVENTURE CENTRE

We got the red card after twenty-four hours.
Fire extinguisher let off in the night,
shop broken into, food reefed off walls.
Too much gowling altogether. At least we got

the trip to the abandoned island: down
a cliff lit with spurge, then the speedboat
slap-batting like a skimmed stone across
the kelp forest staff tried to tell us about.

The lads like the journey but the island
pisses them off. Soon they'll nip off for a smoke,
start firing rocks at birds. Too tired
to care I'm turning a blind eye until

the racket of gulls overhead makes me look down.
The rocky ground is seamed with eggs. Now
we've had it: they'll smash the lot of them,
we'll be abandoned, left here to rot.

Hard to believe what I do hear next:
'I'd be afraid to tread on one of them'.
'You'd never forgive yourself for that, boy'.
'It'd be taking a life, it'd be murder'.

So it happens. The gentled boys remove boots
and tiptoe across the cobbled spine of eggs,
tiptoeing with reverence over the unborn
towards deserted dwellings, the one-way sea.

THE CUP OF TEA

he took her to the dance
and asked her outside
beat her so hard
she nearly died

he made her walk home
with a broken foot
the bone sticking
through her boot

on the good ship Venus

he kept her banged up
for most of her life
she belonged to him
his woman, his wife

she wasn't the same
after number four
left half her womb
on the taxi floor

on the bridge at midnight

he took it from the child
when she was six
held her down while
the uncle dipped his wick

the girl wandered so
he chained her to the floor
she'd not say a word
against him in court

a rum titty tum

THE SILENCE CLOTH

The silence cloth has been laid out
the table's neatly spread
we're using the best china cups
don't mention that he's dead

You've changed the car again I see
it's true what someone said
it's best to change them frequently
don't mention that he's dead

To see exactly what was there
they opened his brave head
do have another sandwich please
don't mention that he's dead

And you must be his brother's son
the one he knew as Fred
a close resemblance certainly
apart from the fact he's dead

Isn't the garden lovely now
that's a lark overhead
I wonder why it sings so much
he can't sing he's dead

he's buried in the potting shed
he's buried in the bed
he's surely going to haunt us all
if we don't say he's dead

he's living in the larder
he's living in the head
he's living in the silence
of not being said to be dead

yes of course you must go now
goodness how time has fled
I'm going to close the door now
and never mention he's dead

TO THE COMMA

minnow dancing through waters of print,
worm at work in the fields of script
bind the body of song

peg for the tents of utterance,
shepherd of phrase and clause
bind the body of song

o stitch in the sentence's sail,
rivet sealing all texts
bind the body of song

HERE

Members of the lesser religions call,
lost salesmen. It's rarely I can help.
Farmers pass by on their way to the bank,
tractors rejoicing every inch of the way.

To these rituals we attend: sugar beet trains
in autumn, the farmgate's one note xylophone,
the polite applause of horseshoes on tarmac.
Herons haunt us. Even the stars look lost.

We don't know what we're doing here at all.
When your mother phones your voice reverts
to geordie, as if you'd never left, as if
we'd never met. There must be some mistake.

At night, the fire takes photographs of us.
Film streams up the chimney, out into
the outside world, straight up to what
we used to know as heaven. Big deal.

It's the sound of geese flying overhead
makes you feel at home. Or was that homeless?

BREAKING GROUND

The digger was breaking an entrance into the garden,
busting down elder and hawthorn scrub, lobbing it
on to a green fire primed with tyres and petrol.
It was a cold summer night, dark and stormy.

Neighbours and I stood hunched in the smoking rain
to appraise the driver's precision. He could take
the tooth out of your mouth with that small bucket;
he could part your hair. Delving into an old midden

each bucketful deserved archaeology. Bedsprings,
they could talk. That teapot could spout forth.
Leg, horse, marriage, record, our talk was all
of breaking until suddenly the digger drove

through and the garden exposed in his headlights
took the words clean out of our mouths. Beaten
down by rain, skulking in shrubs, light hugged
its own poor flesh, as if we had stumbled into

the heart of sorrow, where light grieves
for every broken thing it must shine upon here.
At such a clearing's edge we were trespassers,
only shadow to turn to, and the loss in words.

THE LANDMARK

On the verge, like a clutch of blue eggs,
lay the seven damsons you'd gathered—

dewy, as if they held, for one
moment longer, your last breath.

Sun, on all the known acres, on all
the known stones, like snow fell.

You had grown here like a tree,
taken all this up into you,

streams knew they ran through you,
wind knew the feel of your face,

fields you had learnt and loved
loved themselves under your gaze.

Now those fields are shaken, running
under their boundaries, colliding.

The saw hangs there like a broken wing,
handle palm-silvered, lukewarm.

Grains of sawdust darken in the grass.
Grief wells in the cut trunk's O.

DUNMORE CAVE

When the guide cut the lights
I clutched your hand, cowed
by the weight of dark.

This is the darkest place in Ireland.

Strayed too far down the throat
of the cave, loosestrife cranes
a desperate neck for sun.

Water also is seeking a way out.

Listen: drizzle slinking through
ceiling. Not reaching home.
Air and salt have it stitched.

Committed to the perfect solution.

Sculpting their own dark garden.
Fashioning over aeons this stone limb.
That broken wing. These mailbags.

BAWNREIGH SLATE QUARRY

I

The quarry's a ransacked archive,
broken slate scattered everywhere,
debris left by the hurricane Profit.

Sit here for long you'll hear a flake
fall: the slow keen of slate,
remembering the good old days.

Among the lonely minerals and industries
of Ireland, the quarry's had its day.
It's shattered, brokenhearted, in bits.

Where water's filled the old workings
cliffs peer down on their reflection.
Stand here and shout, slate will hand you

back the perfect echo of your voice.
Here slate is wiping its own slate clean.
Here, for a moment, you might think

slate is mending its broken heart.

II

The Bawnreigh Birdman

Walk out of the air
into the water,
down past the tannery refuse,
down past the rebbidge,

down to where they're still working,
drilling into the slate
to set charges.

This is the last act.
Whether it's bad dynamite
or a spark from a metal bar
it ends in bitterness here—

were they to look up now
they would see me,
sixty years on, swimming
through air one hundred feet
above their heads.

CLAY PIPES

Bits of broken stem
surface now and then,
on which can be read
toothmarks of the dead

fingers packed this bowl
lit it with a coal,
lips closed on this clay
where are those lips today?

clay pipes, gentlefolk
all go up in smoke

underneath the ground
pipes are handed round,
why is the sky blue?
pipesmoke seeping through

the dead breathe us in
we don't come back again,
forget all talk of soul
look in this empty bowl

clay pipes, gentlefolk
all go up in smoke.

MAIN DE GLOIRE

Cut the hand, left or right, from a felon's corpse
hanging on a roadside gibbet. Wrap in winding sheet.
Squeeze tight as possible to drive out any last blood.
For two weeks let it seethe with nitre, salt,
zimort and long peppers, in an earthenware retort.
Dry in an oven heated by fern and vervain.
In the dog days expose to the sun.

Make a candle from virgin wax, Sisamie de Laponie
and a hanged man's fat. Thrust between the fingers
of the hand and light, or use the hand itself,
lighting the thumb and all the fingers.
Now you may steal with impunity: the flame
will prevent sleepers from waking
and stupefy anyone you show it to.

It cannot be blown out by any ordinary person,
nor be extinguished by any liquid save milk.
If the thumb does not catch, beware: someone
is still awake, or unaffected. Do not use where
a threshold is smeared with a black cat's gall,
a white hen's liver or a screech owl's blood. Nor
where there is a large dog, or a burglar alarm.

PALM
after Rilke

Old sole you've gone soft,
too much walking on air.

Sole which on feeling now
learns with feeling to tread.

Meadow of my hand, meadow
which finds other meadows

making with them landscape
filled with meeting.

Palm, calm troubled bed
deep creased by longing,

inner shell shaped to
a fruit formed in prayer.

Broken home of wholeness
by the faraway stars

orphaned and enchanted.

RED HANDED

In the darkness of the church
I felt more than saw. Troubled
shadow, air scratching itself:
a small bird, locked in.

I opened the main door wide.
A bale of warm air fell in,
a cartoon invitation, spiced
with seed and faint sound.

The bird wouldn't buy it.
Over it flew and over against
the sealed chancel windows.
I'd never catch it and yet,

out of its element, estranged,
it seemed somehow we had met.
At length it lay down on
a limestone sill, staring up

at me, resigned. Entreaty
nerved the air between us.
I would carry it down, let it
go into the bright afternoon.

It wouldn't let me touch.
Always at the last moment flew.
There are no safe hands, all
have tasted money, or blood.

HERONS

I

Water stalker, river's eyelash,
when you descended to my pool

you made a fool of yourself,
daft as any god in close up,

twitchy, verminous, uncertain,
out of true in the domestic,

shooed away. Tangled puppet
you gangled up, a squirt

of fishy piss your final word,
open to any interpretation.

Keep that distance now.
Let your far cry bring

jungle to farmland,
prehistory to present.

Be willow by water, be needle
to thread the edges

of sight, seaming those edges
like appetite, prayer.

II

Herons were always here. The one we saw
on the day we moved in seemed an omen.
We named the house for it, wanted
Beware of the Heron painted on the gate.

One gangled often up into the air
off the dyke opposite, a sack of sticks,
almost forgetting its legs, doomed
to crash but finding grace with distance.

Gods need distance. This one stumbled up
from that dyke with one wing pointing
the wrong way. Tried to fly. Fell. Ran
across the field like a frightened child.

For days it skulked in the waterways,
one step ahead of the fox, wing upraised
to ward off the enormous rebuke of sky,
the brightness it had fallen from.

It drew blood when the wildlife ranger
trapped it, folding its gorgeous plumage
in a blanket. He rebroke the wing, set it.
It could have flown, but wouldn't. Starved.

To the ground we returned the standstill
of wing, the stained glass eye, the closed
vowel of stomach, the silence of cry.
All the dried ingredients of grace.

HALCYON

I've never seen the kingfisher
you claim to have witnessed
on the stand of brackish water
at the edge of our wood.

Years I've been looking.
Not a sign. Wrong habitat
too: no bank for nesting,
indeed no fish. Face it

there was no bird yet
each time I pass I peer into
that gloom and each time
this comes to mind:

a flash of chestnutsapphire,
a small flame brooding on ooze.
Your words made light.
Your bright idea. You diving

through the long years
of grief to surface here,
halcyon, incorruptible.
And not one bird but a pair.

SVALA! SVALA!

Just after he moved there, he'd say,
he watched a swallow circle the garden,
widening slowly its orbit until it tapped
with a wingtip at one side a shed window,
at the other passed right under his nose.

At last he went up, opened the window;
sure enough the bird flew straight in.
They had almost spoken.
      'And it built its nest there?'
'No, it rang the week after to say
it had found somewhere cheaper in town.'

He'd drunk away a farm. Was down to
the clothes he stood up in, a radio
for the match, hat like a second skin.
But no one could rob his swallows. Back
they'd come each year, melting out of air

as if, invisibly, they'd been there all along.
He'd swear he knew each individual bird.
They were his luck, his noisy consolation,
but they weren't enough; from the shore
of the sea they brought no wondrous stone.

One autumn, birds he could no longer harbour
whipped dizzyingly through his blood,
hung babbling on the wires of his eyes.
He was found hanging from a rafter,
his eyes empty nests, body a vacant shed.

SNIPE

These soft muds you mine
to your heart's content:
we follow your steps
in the small print.

Puddle skulker,
the ditch your pitch,
it's within earshot
you find your niche,

a chack chickka chackka
rasping through sedge,
the springtime air
rung to its edge

by an air-plucked harp,
your cocked tailfeathers,
a lonely heart ad
for love in the heather.

When nearly trodden on
out you careen,
nothing becomes you
like leaving the scene

rocketted zigzag
off the earth's face
as though speed itself
were a form of grace.

If caught and kept
for just three days
away with our fevers
they say you'd blaze.

[43]

Fly hard or hide
from folklore and gun.
Pilfer the fenland.
Explode into sun.

CONSIDER THE LILIES

Dandelion believes himself
incapable of affection.
Thistle's more lonely than ever.
Ragwort cannot cry.

Stream longs to be a pebble.
Stoat knows he's the only true stoat.
Mountain cannot escape
the hand of his dead father.

Oak's too shy for words.
Grass yearns for a child.
Swallow knows she could be happy
if only, if only.

NOVEMBER

Overnight the sycamore collapses,
leaves black-blistered, cracking into scraps.
The lime tree takes its time, yellows flaming
gently through a pebble lens of mist.

Lifting a stone loose from a wall I find
a mass of snail shells, all quite empty.
Fieldfares racket over after berries.
Gunfire disappears down its own echo.

Across the river, geese are drifting down
to print the inches. Rolled pellets, a wisp
of down, flattened grass are all we can find.
We might be our own ghosts, returning.

Butter of leaves at its feet, the lime stands
astonished, holding nothing up to nothing.

MARSH MARIGOLDS

The leaves go unnoticed most of the year
but chance to glance down in March
you'll see these fat buttery suns glow
in the darkness of dykes like the headlights
of a dense green traffic streaming south.

Carlicups, downscombs, bluddas, johnny cranes,
they go under more than a hundred names
but little do they care as they brighten
like buttons on the suit of a golden giant
asleep in the soft black mud under alders.

APPETITE

The goldfish was basking side-on in the sun,
a fleck of blood in the pond's brown lens.

When it moved I saw pincered inches,
four black beetles padlocked on.

Hungry surgeons, their knives went deep:
white flesh shone against the dark shells.

Mouthing Os of despair, its glamorous face
not framed for pain, the fish was still breathing.

All caught in a net, held up in the air,
the spectacle continued, the beetles feasting,

the fish gasping, until I killed them all.
Even now I can feel those jaws working.

NO PROBLEM

It had started when we kept the fires lit
through the summer, though we didn't know it then.
July lanes blackened by coal lorries
were just something else to moan about.

Winter snow was novel, a good excuse
not to go to work. Sleds were made,
rusted iceskates brought down, new markets
created for thermal jackets, exotic headgear.

When did we first notice that the snow
stayed on the mountains all year round?
That plants were moving down, cloudberry
and three-leaved rush common in the meadows?

When a penguin was seen in Donegal
it just seemed a freak; when more came next year
we felt strangely honoured, singled out.
A special set of stamps was printed.

We soon got used to the icebergs offshore,
the glassy rim thickening beyond the beaches.
Bets are being taken on the chances
of walking across to the neighbouring island,

which still enjoys sunshine we believe.
Some brave souls have skated off already,
hissing into the dark. As yet they've sent
no word, but we know they won't forget us.

They say some areas are cut off completely.
The TV shows only white static, as if
somehow it were speaking on behalf of the cold.
Good will come of it, of that we're certain.

[49]

THE MASKED WALKERS

They are tearing up letters from home.
Not a word must fall into enemy hands.
'I feel that every step in my plan
has been taken with divine help',
writes Haig behind the line. To reflect
sunlight up to the mapping aviators
tin squares are strapped onto packs.
They will go a long way tomorrow.

In Edwardian ease this man trïed,
for a wager, to walk around the world
wearing a mask. He interrupted his journey
for the duration. As night wears off
he's thinking of other world walkers,
Captain Clarke who started out from Yarmouth
sporting a newspaper suit, Arizona Dan
who went dressed as a cowboy.

They'll be beside him today, walking
through the German line onto the open road.
Dazed by the barrage a lark steps into his hand.
He tries to cup what he hopes are its ears.
At the whistle he lays it down
and steps off the parapet, into flowers.
Already it's a beautiful day. 'It's going
to be a walkover', he might have thought.

PORT SUNLIGHT

Charles Lever designed this immaculate hive,
a space for his workers, their children and wives
but the men went to Belgium to fight the good fight
and found their last home in a different light.

THE NEW LIGHT

After a lively evening they retire
to the garden. Pierre displays a tube
partly coated with zinc sulphide,
containing radium in solution.

The Paris night is lit up by particles
thrown off as radium fluoresces
the zinc coat. Light bright enough
to show his hands inflamed and raw.

Hands that could x-ray themselves.
Light-fingered, they break into history.

HONEY

we are pouring honey back into a bucket,
speckled honey, a day's work wasted,

we're strangers plagued by first impressions
awkward, uneasy, needing to get to know,

we've homes to go to, fires to light,
it's gone five o'clock, we've no need to stay

but something in this shared labour lets us
be, until what had seemed so inevitable about

you, about me, seems no more real than rain
pushing down this particular leaf, that chance

angle of light, we're lost in work, nowhere
to be found, birdsong passing through us,

registered, named, but not detained—
not face, not voice, not mind, not self,

just hands pouring honey, wing, wax, pollen,
light, down into a bucket's deepening gold.

THE TAKABUTI MUMMY
Mummy of a married woman
from the 23rd Dynasty, in the Ulster Museum

Under the weight of boredom
her body's turned to stone,
her own stone,
sediment of repetition.

She just can't believe it:
a parcel sent to the sun
only to be opened by Hincks
in rainy Killyleagh,
then to be put on display.

One eye's nearly fallen out.
A brown netting dribbles through.
She's sick of being gawped at,
sick of what she must witness:
centuries of news flashes,
an eternity of repeats.

Everything about her says
we've learnt nothing; her hand
reaches for the off-switch.

*

Look again. From above
she appears to smile.
Her fair hair still
holds its shy light.

Look at her foot. Arched,
intact, it walks on air,
stands for nothing.

Of her fingers three have fused
but the little one's perfect,
like a child's.

Look at the stone fingers
of Amenophis next door,
giant fingers clenched on stone,
all that's left of his giant likeness.

Her hand closes on nothing.
It is not found wanting.

THE SUN ROOM

Six foot of hardcore stood between us and damp
when we moved in, but the dark wouldn't budge.
Even after we'd cleared their sills of relics, windows
seemed hostile to light, loth to give it floorspace.

So we broached the endwall, built a glass room,
a great wound of light which reached into every corner.
And all summer we were home and dry, photocopied
by the kind sun, but in autumn our breaths began

to fog the glass, dripping back down onto our food.
Now the steady blade of a dehumidifier bales up
every drop of moisture. I wait for the red light
to announce it's full, waiting to collect each

liquid ingot, each bright pint full of us.
Could they reconstruct our lives from these—
our shining, inconsequential archives? I carry
the container to the sink, start to pour, Moses

woken from a bad dream, arms full of water and light.

LETTER FROM LADAKH

Nights are so long without you
though I hold heaven in my arms
in a silence that reaches to Russia.

Learning the art of non-attachment
proves hard. It is good to share
my life with you: distance seems
to make us closer and who's to say
now where I end, where you begin?

Truth is if I cannot sleep with you
I cannot sleep without you, so I lie
awake, rehearsing what I've seen:
white thistles in a downpour of light,
old cans used to protect the trunks
of young trees, the way night
folds away mountains to disclose
the simple, kind machinery of stars.

Everything's alright then, so it seems,
but the meditation's a dead loss.
I can't sit in the right position,
my back's killing me, I can't concentrate,
can't stop relating all this to you.

Water's always looking for the quickest
way out of this high and dry land.
Its sound seems to sharpen the silence.
That's how I've seen our attachment:
sound as the ring on a finger of silence.

'You went a long way to find that out',
I hear you say. I know, fine words butter
no parsnips, you didn't come up the Tyne

on a bike. 'Far be it from me to demur',
I'm muttering aloud, in that smarmy way
I think I know you love to hate.

CATCHING THE LIGHT

Over Gortrush Wood, low on the horizon,
an orange husk of moon.
One star burning in the last wash of sunlight
higher in the sky.
All still but for the hum of a generator,
odd twang of a snipe.

Soil sleeps on its bed of rock. Moths might be
flakes of wood
on the housewall. Skins of dark form
over skins of dark
and all are caught in my net of sight,
both me and what I see.

Medusas, my eyes: what they say they see
my tongue has no choice
but to confirm. No slipping the tongue.
No such thing as no idea.
Moon. Wood. Horizon: habits of a lifetime,
words made flesh

but what seems to lie beyond them tonight seems
not emptiness but
light, or what we call light. Not to be grasped,
not to be spilt.
Moon, wood, horizon: made of light.
Moth, snipe: light.

In a world of light we are creatures of distinction
lost and found
as we speak. Lost and found at this given moment
in the wonder of saying
an orange husk of moon low on the horizon
over Gortrush Wood.

UNBECOMING

For too long he has stood at your door,
this small bewildered boy, fringe hung
over national-health specked eyes,
timbertongued boy, unworthy of mention.

For too long in his only mirror,
your eye, he has seen himself
othered, ambered, pupilled, only meal
in that eye's desert his own tears.

It is time to let him in. Time
to sit him down and serve him.
Take off your arms. Take out your eyes.
Enter his mouth. Loosen his tongue.

Listen. All his life he has loved you.
Take his word. Onto his heart graft your heart.

PRAYER

How we survive, Lord. Twenty two homes,
sixteen schools before we were ten.
Those blind uncles touching us up.
Our wounds wide open, our words not heard
until we wept, but were not allowed to.
O the tears uncried strained against
the eyes, the good conduct medals.

It's no wonder, Lord. Fingers at
the underwear, fists in the stomach,
stories spooled inside us, pleading
to be repeated. Look at us, crawling
from the wrecks of our childhoods,
begging any stranger for a hug.
O what happened. And what happened.

Let us praise, tonight, ourselves.
Our flesh, bones, eyes, hands, hair,
the brightness of our being.
How should our light not shine?
Look at us, Lord, praise us,
real tonight as each other,
as real as can be. Beyond belief
our beauty, our right to be here.

INSTINCT

After a week of talk to walk
into the garden's empty air
and become, by working, my hands.

To follow the turn of those hands
into the garden's instinct, means
by which it makes and mends itself

and by doing what needs to be done
for mind to settle and clear,
a home for the slightest of sounds.

To hold and be held by soil's
dark hands, to know the air
so still a leaf might fall

forever and to feel that leaf
fall slowly right through me.
To be with air by darkness veined,

to reap and be the evening's fruit,
Air, Bird, Garden, Star.
Air, Bird, Garden, Star.

Do not call me now I am
water in a glass of silence.
Do not call, I am uncontained.

PRACTICE

Tired perhaps from work
early in the week
across the dropping dark
we gather in the church.

First breathing exercise
to open the lungs' doors,
mee-may-mah-mow-moos
to sharpen vocal claws

then hard graft on the score,
our voices awkward birds
groping for the footwork
to grip the music's perch

laying down a path
over shafts of breath,
teaching mind and mouth
to make notes by heart

as if the tongue
all throats being one
instead of singing
found itself sung

as if into the air
selves could disappear
fuel of a choir
become a single fire

as if beyond poise
lay a kind of grace
where the human voice
becomes blossoming space.

Descent from height
is a law of flight.
Wrapped again in coats
we head into the night.

As the road unwinds
it's back to routine.
Thoughts start to churn
in the mind's daft machine

but in bed, close to sleep
you find that mind swept,
blown like a pipe
by notes you can't stop

WHAT THE DEER SAID

I am my shyness, said the deer.
I am not searching for common ground.
I do not need to be cured.

What makes me tremble so?
The world's infinite sweetness,
sweetness by fear ripened.

Not our song but our silence
passes all understanding.
And we are silent when we sing.

If love can be a measure of distance
grant me that distance.
I am my shyness. Love my shyness.

TO SILENCE

Silence, on the mountain we can almost see
your hands fold around insect and bird,
fasten on the wake of the wind.
The higher we climb the higher you rise.

High clear sound you love:
a sheep bell, the call of a chough
you linger over and cherish,
stretch out across yourself
until they form a coat, a tent,
a small home in the air for you.
Reluctantly you let them fall,
skin by skin, ghost inside ghost
diminishing.

In the highest valleys you worship
and are worshipped by water,
its constant slap across stone
a mirror you see yourself in,
a string you play yourself on.

On your face we paint our gods.

Perhaps the deepest longing you feel:
there are those who burrow into you,
who stay in you until you start
to listen and open and make for them
inside yourself a cave, your listening
a form of love, a meeting.

Your job is the washing of worlds,
you whom we journey through and join.
In your hand, wider than the universe,
silence hold my hand.

SCYTHE

Come with me into the barn.
Feel, first, the cold space, how
it enters into wall and floor

and how this cold space humbles,
peels away stock feeling
to leave you in a new place.

Take the scythe down from its hook.
Weigh the strange trembly blade,
know it only finds poise in motion.

Take it outside, into the darkness.
Brace yourself. So. Start to swing.
Imagine: you are reaping silence.

Bright sheaves of silence.
With each swing watch them fall.
Work hard to keep the rhythm, work

until the scythe swings itself.
Now look back. Find those sheaves
not fallen at all but sprung

again, unbroken, multiplying
and you the reaper cutting
your way to the field's core.

Do not look for absolutes.
You will hear many small noises,
you will hear your own blood

but should you hear a rook call
understand it as a finger
on the lips of silence.

Work until you are being worked,
until there is only you and the scythe,
until there is neither you nor scythe

until there is only what there is.